Ralph's Poetry

&

Music

Dedication

To my Loving Mother

Rosia Mae Gandy

&

My Children

Deborah D. Gates

Donna D. Wilkerson

Dayatra D. Arnold

D'Shawn D. Watts

&

Nephew

Jimmy Hawkins

A Word from the Author

Many people are seeking the truth
Many believe they know the truth but
Carries a heavy burden.

A heavy burden makes one undesirable,
Repulsive and untrustworthy. Then he
Becomes confined in a state of hate,
Greed and animosity.

No one can be successful in their findings
Until they recognize and part from
This confinement.

How?
LOVE, PRODUCTIVITY and FAITH

LOVE-make one desirable; this puts him
at the door of worthyship.

PRODUCTIVITY-knocks on the door of worthyship
and you will find KUW. (Means) knowledge,
Understanding and Wisdom. These are the tools
mankind must possess to perform his duties.

FAITH-this is his credential. Without credit

there is little hope. This is your Assurance

of Emancipation. Your liberation from

burdens and difficulties in life.

by

Ralph L. Watts

A Proverb

Think not of yesteryears
Its deteriorate the brain
With forgotten tears

By
Ralph L. Watts

Side of the Road

By

Ralph L. Watts

Here I stand on the side of the road
Scorned thru days and nights of cold
Brutalized by conditions often in despair
Criticized by the fortunate, to roads lead elsewhere

My future is uncertain, all bills are unpaid
Distress by the brain, overworked, tense, hair fully grayed
Depressed by the strain, evidence of heavy loads
Please don't leave me on the side of the road.

Oh! Disappearing friends and prosperous diplomats
With perforated minds, fame and truth to combat
Celebrating unclean fortunes; proudly as you strode
Neglecting the innocence on the side of the road.

My legs are weak and a reat feel of thirst
My eyes for sleep, understanding at its worst
Misfit, unfit, scum, no good, all I been told
Located here on the side of the road.

Oh God! Suspend my death, preserve my faith!
Purify my breath, your word I'll never forget
I'm still, fulfill, thrill, your grace I behold
Patiently waiting here on the side of the road.

Copyright 1984
ISBN 0-88147-008-2
ISSN 0734-5135

I Thank Thee

By
Ralph L. Watts

I thank thee Father for the love
And blessings appearing year after year
The sun, the moon shines from above
The bullet unsped, the unshed tear.

I thank thee for the lie untold
The enemy that missed its prey
The upcoming fate and weary soul
The clean hearts with joy and gay.

I thank thee Father for the care
Given to the young and old
The thirst, the hunger I did not share
No disease, no illness in this body I hold.
I thank thee for life itself
Everything on land, air and sea
You, I and everything left
Your loyal to all and things to be.

Copyright 1994
ISBN 1-881808-10-6

Old Raggedy House

By
Ralph L. Watts

Thanks for this old raggedy house
Quiet, peaceful, even without a mouse
Weather changes bring a little pain
That cold wind and summer rain.

Rags and paper plugged in the holes
Does a good job keeping out the cold
Ooh! Here comes a hard rain!
Pots and pans! Again and again!
Catching all the water I can

Copyright 1993
ISBN 1-56167-049-9

Distant Run

Securing a sound education is a long distant run
Compounding knowledge, conserving fortitude out-weighs a ton
Ambitious to perform and endure a long worth-while mission
Dedicated to learning, fairplay, worship and continuous competition.

Any Distant Run conquered; one must be glad
This consistent motivation, profitable for any lad
Utilizing conditions, cultivating problems makes a prime candidate
Finish your run! I promise success waits.

Completing any Distant Run is to your advantage
It improves sanity and provides security in old age
The bumps and lumps prices must be paid
Only superb craftsmanship ups and maintains the grade.

Don't underestimate the stones, bridges and pathways of fabrication
Dedicate and perform true merits is the bridge of graduation
Master the bests! Attack the hardships! Be someone!
Awards wait at the finish line of your Distant Run.

A Vote for me

By
Ralph L. Watts

It matters much who back I scratch
Or agree on unethical contracts
I prefer defeat than to unlatch
Allegations I can't subtract.

A vote for me provides the key
To unlock justice and restore order
Placing moral values where they should be
By freeing hope and respect for our elders.

Opportunity stands here on this stage
Caged with truth, hope and virtues of men
Your vote for me unlocks this cage
Fulfilling our lives once again.

A vote for me promising you
Honest, constant undefiled workmanship
Decisions directed to your point of view
Satisfying a need long over due.

We need a change and don't forget
Your chance is now! You're at the top
So make the change, you want regret
Remember my name at the ballot box.

School

By
Ralph L. Watts

Up in the mornings, going to school
Receiving an education for my basic tool
Studying hard, earning good grades
While my buddies playing in the arcade.

When I pass, they call me a fool
While shooting pool and acting cool
Its hurts some, to be called names
Today; without an education is a darn shame.

To you who play hooky from school
And those sitting around on bar stools
Laugh on! Call me a cheap skate
But I plan to make it! And make it straight.

Back to the pool with the jitty-bugs
Slipping 'round and using drugs
Boys! You better cut that out!
You're prison bound and that's no doubt.

I don't like to attract attention
But these few words I must mention
Go to school! Don't be a square!
Without an education, you gets no-where.

Mountain Top

By
Ralph L. Watts

Oh Mountain Top how do you do?
Quietly standing, giving a wonderful view
Midst a halo of cloud curled to a veil
with the rising sun giving every detail.

Your repose head reigns in the sky
Maintains beauty as centuries go by
Innocence, confidence yet full of suspense
Solidly based with no false pretense.

Misbehaved man says you cheat
Making their graves at your feet
I think you are sweet...
competitor and a sound athlete.

You want say, your thoughts are concealed
Mysteries, knowledge, you want reveal
I often wonder "Who is your architect"?
Could God in heaven make a prime suspect?

O'er Thur Hill

(From an old man)

Lotta people sae ium o'er thur hill
Thar horsh voises brant outh tells
Somma tham sae ium almuss N ma grave
I mite cee a stone weth thar neme ingrave

I donce thenk mush uv ma ege
Du Gode an tiem I tri tu seve
Imma ole man till goen tu werk
Payen tackes, taken kair uv thom jerks.

Some mornen I hava little backaka
Wril werking I meka sum mestakes
I rather be o'er ther hill earnen ma meels
Then undur ther hill, kough trien tu steel.

Yeah! Ium o'er ther hill an free
An gonna tell, whet u ott notta be
Layen round pranken an haven drenks
Butt werk, go benken an geve God thenks.

Winter Wind

By
Ralph L. Watts

Oh! Winter Wind thou are unseen
Producing chills with breath so keen
Over the land and over the sea
Moving swiftly, stinging like a bee.

You are often angry when you come
Attacking breeze freezes, make some numb
Some to cry and some to die
Others are waiting to say goodbye.

Constantly moving supplying severe cold
To the rich, poor, young and old
I don't think we have a choice
Your voice we listen and try to rejoice.

You must reign from coast to coast
Galloping gallantly and playing host
Conflicting pain as a raging knight
A foe you are thru-out the night.

I Am Afraid

I'm afraid to be tested or examine at a trail
To face one robed in black with a mask of injustice
Innocence doesn't matter, horror waits in the dark
Satan about to serenade, pernicious as a shark.

What happen to innocence? There's no proof of guilt
Innocence is enclosed like cloth to a quilt
Corrupted and unjust minds, where must I find aid?
Truth is gone, incompetent inclined, see why I'm afraid.

Who is responsible? Why am I afraid?
The innocent tormented, punished with evidence not full weighed
This mischievous unpardonable sin, some courts have Okayed
It's a disgrace! It's tragic! Yes I am Afraid.

Oh disease of injustice! You became an epidemic
Contagious to dishonor, incompetent and needs a gimmick
Destroying productive minds, suffering to all mankind
I Am Afraid you left truth and honesty behind.

You are truly guilty and should be punish
Double the agony to others you have furnish
Help somebody! The truth he will evade
Patiently waiting for I am Afraid.

PIANO SCORE

FROM THE MUSICAL LIBRARY OF:
RALPH L. WATTS

"UNFORGETABLE"

WORDS AND MUSIC BY: RALPH L. WATTS
ARRANGED BY: C. STERN, &
C. BATTON

COPY/ C. BATTON: FOR MUSIC '86

© COPYRIGHT BY RALPH L. WATTS 1984

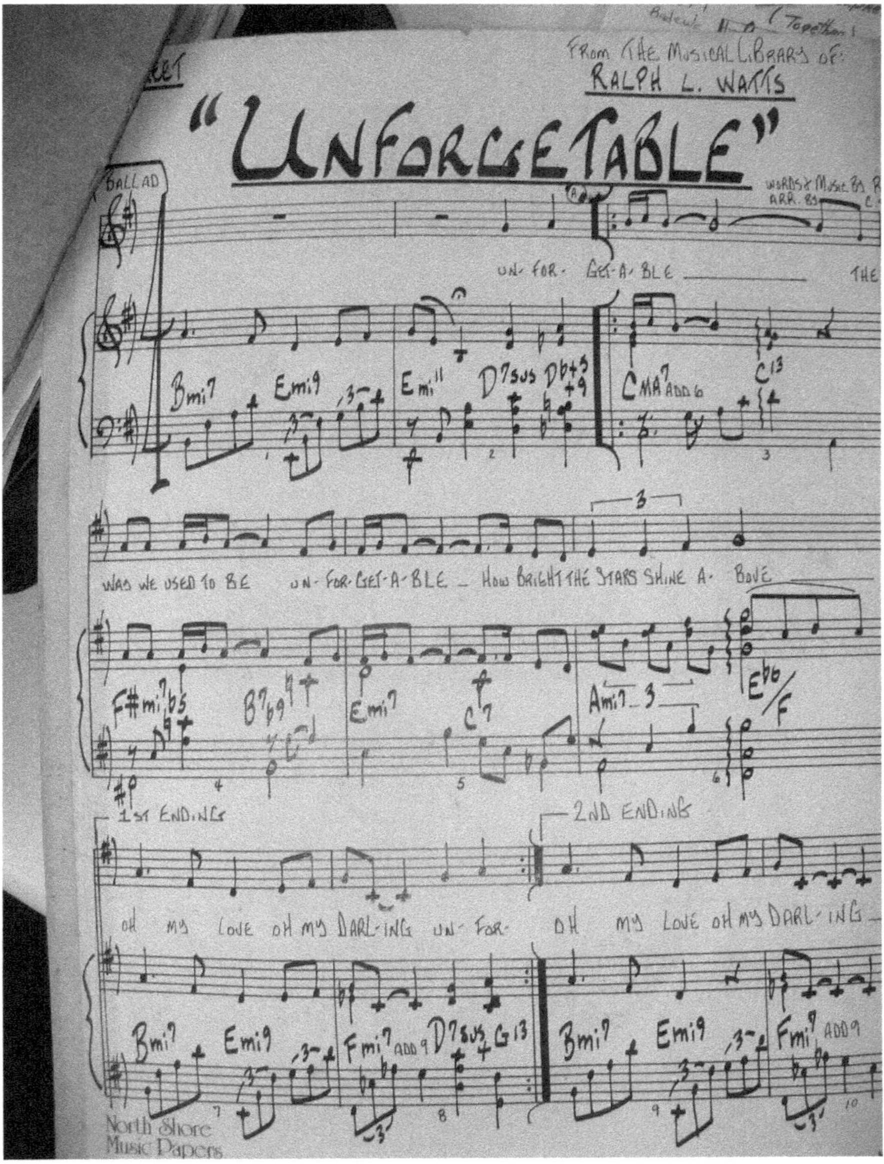

FROM THE MUSICAL LIBRARY OF:
RALPH L. WATTS
"UNFORGETABLE"
BALLAD
UN-FOR-GET-A-BLE
THE
WAS WE USED TO BE UN-FOR-GET-A-BLE HOW BRIGHT THE STARS SHINE A-BOVE
1ST ENDING
2ND ENDING
OH MY LOVE OH MY DARL-ING UN-FOR-
OH MY LOVE OH MY DARL-ING
North Shore
Music Papers

- 2 -

How could you forget me_____ How could you ever come to be Un-pre-

dict-a-ble_____ You left me when we were doing fine to-get-her Un-pre-dict-a-ble_____

Why'd you leave with an-oth-er_____ Oh, my love my darling_____

(Timothy) C

HOW COULD WE LEAVE EACH OTH-ER ___ UN-FOR-GET-A-BLE ___ HOW I
Ami7 GMA7 Emi7
Bbmi7
Eb MA9
Ami9
Bmi7
WAIT-ED ___ AND WAIT-ED ___ TO SEE YOU ___ UN-FOR-GET-A-BLE ___ HOW
C7#11
Bmi7
Ami7
Emi7
Ami11
CMA7
A7 SUS4
YOU STAYED A-WAY LIKE YOU NE-VER KNEW OH MY LOVE OH MY
Cmi7
A13 Bmi7
Bbmi7
Eb7
Emi7
A7

32
33
34
35
Copy/C. Batton: For Music '86
CLYDE BATTON
ACCOUNT #50428
LOCAL 10-208, A.F. of M.
COPYIST DEC 29, 1986

UNFORGETABLE

Ballad

Words + Music By Ralph L. Watts

1. un-for-get-a-ble, the way we used to love, un-for-get-a-ble, how bright the
2. un-for-get-a-ble, the way we used to be, un-for-get-a-ble, the way you

stars shine above— oh my love, oh my darling how could you ever forget me—
made love to me— oh my love oh my darling how could this ever come to be—

un-pre-dict-a-ble—, you left while doing well to-geth-er— un-pre-dict-a-ble, how

you left with an-oth-er— oh my love, my darling—how could we leave each other.

un-for-get-a-ble— how I waited and waited to see you un-for-get-a-ble—

How you stayed a-way like you never knew, oh my love—my darling—

how could I ever forget you—.

© 1984 By Ralph L. Watts

© 1984 Ralph L. Watts   Pau 1-24-433

1984 By Ralph L. Watts
Words + Music
Ralph L. Watts
P.O. Box 9707
LOVE PAINS
1. Your Love it Pains dear, each Time You call
2. our love Was once True, All the day thru
When You com-plains Fear,
Noth-ing to do but,
3. What Made our Love Go, I Just don't know
4. Your Love it Pains dear, Thru night of cold
But I've Got Love Pains,
I Can't ex-plain and, No
Knows.
MORE

"I'm Surprised" — Duet, Slowly, with expression — By Ralph L. Watts

(Together) chorus

I'm sur-prised. ____ I'm sur-prised. ____ I'm sur-prised. ____ I'm sur-prised. ____ To Verses

(Male) When we first met I did-n't re-al-ize. ____ Love at first sight I could not be-lieve. ____ For-ev-er it shall be. You I nev-er de-ceive ____ Repeat Chorus

(Female) Be-ing with you makes my life worth liv-ing ____ my be-loved your faults, all is for-giv-ing. ____ I'll do my best the rest of my life. I'm sur-prised your words so var-y nice. ____ Repeat Chorus

(Male) I'm sur-prised this love-ly voice I hear. ____ When-ev-er we sang, feel-ings bring a tear. ____ Those sur-pris-ing tears makes your beau-ty charms. ____ Com-for-ta-ble I feel while in your arms. Repeat Chorus

(Cont.)

Surprised

By Ralph L. Watts

(Together) with you in my arms, no-thing I have to say, my love for you is
here to stay.— To-geth-er, for-ev-er. High on the sun-rise. I'm sur-
prised.— I'm sur- prised. —— I'm sur- prised—— I'm sur-
prised. — I'm sur-

Repeat And Fade.

We Love The Country

WORDS + MUSIC BY Ralph L. Watts

1984 By Ralph L. Watts
Nationwide Music Co.

BRISKY

We Get up mornings fore sun rise To feed the cows and hogs

And before we Re-a-lize As Time goes out The Boys...

Tween cutting Logs and working Fields we find Time To hunt for coons...

will do all This To Save a Dollar Bill If it means looking by The moon...

We Love The Country With loads of sand And dest y-

(Chorus)

DREAMS

Ev-e-ry night I go to bed sweet dreams come to my head Yours is
on-ly face I see When dreams take place To-mor-row I will feel
bet-ter the whole day thru Just thinking of you Oh dreams pl
come True Ev-e-ry time I lay my head dreams wait-ing on my bed
hold-ing and loving you The whole night thru Oh dreams please come Tru
Dreams al-ways on the scene Night-ly love is your rou-tine as I be-g
To hug Sun-light pulls the plug Oh dreams Please come True.
Dreams al-ways on my bed Wait-ing for my head To hold and love
the whole night thru Dreams, dreams dreams
(Fade)

©1984 By Ralph L. Watts

"A GOOD YEAR"

BY RALPH L. WATTS

[BALLAD]

LET'S MAKE THIS A GOOD YEAR, HOLD-ING YOU IN MY ARMS. HOP-ING YOU'LL AL-WAYS BE NEAR.

LET'S MAKE THIS A GOOD YEAR, TO-GETHER OUR LOVE WILL IND, AND BE HEARD, BY EV-RY EAR.

CAR-EER I WON'T IN-TER-FERE, IF HELP IS NEED-ED I'LL -UN-TEER. I LOVE YOU DON'T YOU SEE,

NEV-ER BEEN, SO SIN-CERE, NO MAT-TER HOW THINGS AP-EAR. WE'RE GON-NA MAKE, THIS A GOOD YEAR.

NEV-ER WANT-ED TO BE FREE, TO-GETHER IN LOVE WE DO A-GREE, A GOOD YEAR FULL OF HAR-MO-NY.

1984 By Ralph L. Watts P.O. Box 9707, Jax, FL 32208 (904) 268-7929

DREAMING

Chorus (f)	Dreaming_____dreaming_____dreaming_____
(chorus bkgd p)	Everynight I got to bed Sweet dreams come to my head Yours is the only face I see when dreams take place.
Chorus (f)	Dreaming_____ ___dreaming_____dreaming_____
	Everytime I lay my head Dreams waiting on my bed Holding and loving you Oh dreams! Please come true____
	Darling you don't understand How I feel holding your hand Makes me dream that satisfieds And keeps you by my bedside__.
Chorus (f)	Dreaming____dreaming_____dreaming_____.
	Dreaming all thru the night You and I making things right As I began to hug____ Sunlight pulls the plug_____
	Every morning when I rise My dreams are the prise They carry me thru the day Hoping they want go away_____
Fade	Dreaming, dreaming, dreaming, etc.

Ralph L. Watts
P.O. Box 9707
Jax, FL 32208
(904)766-7123

FORGIVE ME (male vocalist)

Forgive me, yes darling, please forgive me
I love only you don't you see
Don't end our love these words I plead
Please forgive me your wishes is guaranteed.

I were wrong overlooking your love
You are my own, forever my belove
My success, my future you are the key
I can't rest, darling please forgive me.

I've been accused of having an affair
Giving me the blues, heartaches and nightmares
I don't agree you want to be free
Down on my knees, please for-give me.

Forgive me, your needs I will provide
Forgive me, our future you will decide
I love only you these words I plea
Make our life anew, please forgive me.

Ralph L. Watts
P.O. Box 9707
Jax, FL 32208
(904)768-7123

I CAN'T FORGIVE

NO! NO! NO! You I can't forgive
Your love for me, you did not give
No need to plead, your words are negative
You ignored my wishes, this I can't forgive.

Overlooking my love , once you are correct
You became a bum and lost all respect
My love, life, all I had to give
Sliced with your knife, I can't forgive.

About that affair, with that other chic
I had the nightmares, thought of giving arsenic
You had no blues but played the avenues
I can't forgive nor want any rendezvous.

Let this message be your signpost
On every corner from coast to coast
No more lies, tries, whys or alibi's
Tearing eyes, cries, stop no goodbyes.

Keep that slick chic, I'll hold the arsenic
I have the antidote, don't miss this boat
My life I shall live, I have the motive
Things are affirmative, no, I can't forgive.

Ralph L. Watts
P.O. Box 9707
Jax, FL 32208
(904)768-7123

I LOVE THE COUNTRY

I love the country
    with roads of sand and dusty
No better place to live
    with nothing we got to give.

We get-up mornings 'fore sunrise
    to feed the cows and hogs
And before we realize
    it time to cut the logs.

'tween cutting logs and working fields
    we find time to hunt 'coons
We do all this to save a dollar bill
    if it means working by the moon.

(chorus)

We can't afford to get up late
    or stand under the tree shade
There'll be no food for my plate
    or products we can trade.

(chorus and fade)

                                        Ralph L. Watts
                                        P.O. Box 9707
                                        Jax, FL 32208
                                        (904)768-7123

CENTRAL CITY PLAYBOY

Oh central city playboy
        so full of fun and joy
I'm ma tak-u out to the country
        and get your pants a little dusty.

Hey central city playboy
        back home they called me Leroy
I'm out to dusty your pants
        and make you crawl like ants.

'cause I'm from the country
        "U" say we are always dusty
I'm here to cut that fun
        so don't you try to run.

Bang! Bang! Bang!

Sorry central city playboy
        That's my brother Troy
One thing you didn't know
        the way he says hello.

I'm going back to the country
where roads are sandy "N" dusty
Playing my guitar, singing my song
"cause my work here is done.

Loving You

Loving you_____
        from our very first date
        I promise to go straight
        My love will be true
        always to you————————

Holding you_____
        in my arms I realize
        our love was organize
        and forever be justified
        being at each other's side

Loving you_____
        the whole night thru
        like we never knew
        there are no tomorrows
        or ends to rainbows

Wanting you_____
        the rest of my life
        to be by your side
        with nothing to fear
        year after year____

Loving you_____
        makes me feel much better
        to understand and forever
        my whole life I'll give
        as long as I live_____

Ralph L. Watts
P.O. Box 9707
Jax, FL 32208
(904)768-7123

Ralph L. Watts
P.O. Box 9707
Jax, FL 32208
(904) 768-7123

SITTING 'round THE BARN

This is a story about an old farmer, who love to sit
around the barn.

As he was sitting one evening; an old friend came by
and this is what he had to say.

"Howdy! Pull up that old chair and beware; what I'm
about to say haven't been told anywhere"

The old friend pulls up a chair nearby.
(he went on)
"I love sitting 'round this barn thinken 'bout ma farm.
I should curse 'coase things can't get worse. I'm swal-
lowing ma pride, these things I can't hide" (pause)

"I committed no crimes ma whole lifetime. Maybe a little
gin but they said that was no sin"

"Out there are rows with nothing to sow. No need for this
hoe when nothing want grow. There is no grain 'cause it
didn't rain"

"Ma hogs I need but can't feed. Deeply in debt, yet, I go
to church; although not very much. No one claim to be a
saint, I know I ain't. I've been baptized and advised, seek
not to be rich. Now all I need is a sandwich" (tears falls)

"Don't mine these tears, they are years of hard labor in
fields which very little yielded"

"Ma wife looking thru the window, trying to ignore the
house for sale. Well; looks like I've failed" (wipe tears)

more

SITTING 'round THE BARN

"Ma condition is critical! All day I haven't ate,
saving food for ma mate. We have a little to eat
but no meat. Some gingerbread I saved is in the
shed!'

"I'm filled with fright and nothing in sight. Ma
appetite is dangling like a foe in the night!'

"So ma friend, I'm here waiting for the end. In
this old chair, no better place anywhere—SITTING
'ROUND THE BARN!'

Ralph L. Watts
P.O. Box 9707
Jax, Fl 32208
(904)768-7123

May God continue blessing you.

Author

www.ingramcontent.com/pod-product-compliance
Lightning Source LLC
Chambersburg PA
CBHW030010040426
42337CB00012BA/718